Hitler's Youth and Rise

By: Eduardo R Riusech

Hitler's Youth and Rise

The idea that a man can go from a modest beginnings to the highest powers of a very tight nit government like Germany during the early part of the 20th century is incredible to say the least. The understanding of Hitler's youth to his early political ambitions also tell the story of how a Austrian boy became the leader of Germany. It is important to focus on the different world events that affected him directly from the death of his parents to political revolution all the way to entering power to fully understand how every part of his leadership was a run away train in the making.

Hitler's parents were named Alois and Klara Hitler[1]. Hitler's father adopted the name because of a very rustic family name that did not suit him for his desire to climb the ladder of Austrian social service. Hitler's father was born in a very poor and wooded area near Bohemia. He did not receive mass amounts of education although his inner desire to better his circumstance would push him to civil service and eventually as a customs agent for the Austrian government.

In the family dynamic Hitler's father, Alois was the disciplinarian that wished his son to follow in his footsteps and civil service. Hitler's father figured that joining civil service was the sole reason for his family to reach the middle class; it would benefit the continued rise of this family for his son to continue on in that tradition. Hitler himself excelled in primary school and had few problems in education until his father decided to put him in a more progressive

---

[1] Kershaw, Ian. *Hitler*. 2nd ed. Vol. 1. New York: W.W. Norton, 1999.

school in Linz. Klara, Hitler's mother[2], was very caring, and in some ways overly so towards her son Adolf. The reading describes Hitler's mother as a very, it will lack of a better term, touchy-feely and supporting mother.

The household dynamic could not be more polar opposites. Hitler's father being a strict disciplinarian pusher of education, and a proponent of government service, while Hitler's mother was a overly gullible and passionate mother that allowed her son to do just about anything he wanted[3]. It is understood and the many times explained in the reading that the mixture between both extremes let Hitler to his later hardline narcissistic beliefs. It is hard for me to support such an idea considering that many people grow up with the idea of a dual-purpose

---

2 Jetzinger, Franz. *Hitler's Youth*. London: Hutchinson, 1958.

3 Kershaw, Ian. *Hitler*. 2nd ed. Vol. 1. New York: W.W. Norton, 1999.

family where one parent is a disciplinarian and the other is what would be known as the emotional contributor[4]. Few people in history have even come close to matching Hitler's atrocities.

I believe a good reason for this is because the abilities of the German people in industry and innovation. If Hitler would have led a less advanced culture, he would more likely not been able to accomplish the things that he did and will World War II.

In fact, many see through the reading Hitler's father and the actions and starting positions that he took with his military and political leaders.

Early in Hitler's youth, his father passed away which left his mother an overly compassionate woman that allowed Hitler to live it, virtually, discipline free youth in control of the household. Hitler soon quit school in

---

4 Jetzinger, Franz. *Hitler's Youth*. London: Hutchinson, 1958.

order to lead a very carefree life. One that his mother rarely tried to curve, with one that was to include painting, listening of favorite composers, and nightlife.

The interesting part of Hitler's younger years is his detachment from the opposite sex. He noticed beautiful women around him, and with the nightlife that he adopted in his teenage years, would have blossomed possible relationships opportunities, he found himself very alone with the company of a lifelong friend from his hometown of Linz.

Since both of Hitler's parents had passed away by his mid-teens, he lived in an apartment with his lifelong friend. Hitler being the outflow in his friendship always betrayed a life of success in accomplishing his goals[5]. This could not be farther from the truth considering that he had dropped out of high school and other than painting showed little to

---

[5] Jetzinger, Franz. *Hitler's Youth*. London: Hutchinson, 1958.

no interest in any other aspect of life other than that my life of going to the theater to see his favorite composers.

Many around Hitler would explain that regardless of how he portrayed his life he was one of solitude and extreme loneliness[6]. Money given to him by family members controlling the benefits he received from being an orphan child was the sole income he had to sustain himself. His sister living with an aunt also receives these benefits, however Hitler's aunt required him to attempt to acquire some sort of an education. Hitler told his aunt back in Linz that he was studying to gain admission into an Academy of Art[7].

Art definitely was Hitler's lifelong ambition. Living in Geneva, he had tried on three separate

---

6 Jetzinger, Franz. *Hitler's Youth*. London: Hutchinson, 1958.

7 Kershaw, Ian. *Hitler*. 2nd ed. Vol. 1. New York: W.W. Norton, 1999.

occasions to gain admission to the school of arts there. He did fairly well on the entrance examinations failing solely in the last part of admission were in one instance he was even told by one of the professors that Hitler indeed had a gift but one that led more towards architecture rather than fine art[8]. The biggest problem that Hitler faced was that since he had dropped out of school he had no formal education in which he would be able to proceed with a curriculum and studying architecture. For some time Hitler explained to his family back home that he was simply finishing his education in order to gain admission to the arts Academy to study architecture. In theory this would've been a wonderful idea for Hitler, however he made no attempt in finishing his education in order to accomplish what you told his family he was going to do.

---

[8] Kershaw, Ian. *Hitler*. 2nd ed. Vol. 1. New York: W.W. Norton, 1999.

Hitler seemed content merely letting the lie and going through this small inheritance provided by the government. Even those closest to Hitler did not grasp the fabrication of what was Hitler's life in Vienna. After some short time, Hitler's best friend was living with him decided to go back home since his education had come to an end. This made living his life almost completely impossible. Hitler now did not have the luxury of his expenses being split and therefore caused Hitler to live a life of solitude and poverty even though it was self-imposed.

In the reading Hitler explains how much he disliked Vienna however no matter how bad things got there made no attempt to return home to the remainders of his family and the attempts at improving his situation. Hitler merely existed, not taking advantage of any of the circumstances nor vice that he had received from either family or professors at the Art Institute. It is very difficult for one to understand why a young Hitler would not concede to his inability to manage his own life situation and attempt to be guided by someone in order to improve the situation. This I think shows the incredible ego that he had throughout his life that made it virtually impossible for him to make any positive decisions in order to improve on virtually any decision he made throughout his life.

Hitler then became a resident at a boarding house simply painting in order to make a living[9]. The interesting situation, is that the hatreds that would come out later in Hitler's political views still up to this point had not manifested and would not do so completely until the end of World War I. Although it is clear that while living in the boarding house he did receive an introduction to speaking and different

---

9 Shirer, William L. *The Rise and Fall of Adolf Hitler*. New York: Random House, 1961.

political ideology provided by many of the obscure individuals who live there.

Hitler was so detached from what he was to become that much of his day-to-day dealings were with people that he would later condemn as Europe's worst enemies.

One cannot discuss Hitler's putsch attempt without discussing his participation in World War I and what led to his dissolution of the German government. Hitler served with distinction in World War I, for the first time showing promise in a profession that had long lasted in time compared to other professions he tried[10]. Hitler was not automatically allowed to join the German army because of his financial issues holding him in Austria. The reading indicates either a mixture of need for

---

10 Shirer, William L. *The Rise and Fall of Adolf Hitler*. New York: Random House, 1961.

soldiers or leniency based on the fact that he was volunteering for the Army allowed certain things to be overlooked, which placed Hitler as a corporal in the German military.

He showed great resolve and fortitude and was even awarded highly decorated awards in Germany while serving. Interestingly enough he did not hold rank of any significant importance that would indicate any specific leadership trait to expand past any particular mission that he undertook[11]. Since he was a corporal was hard-pressed to imagine that he was given any tests or missions of great importance that would indicate that Hitler would show great military promises. On the other hand he did show a talent on the battlefield for carrying out orders but never be in a position to actually giving orders himself. I would've thought that this epiphany would have more of a

---

[11] Kershaw, Ian. *Hitler*. 2nd ed. Vol. 1. New York: W.W. Norton, 1999.

lasting impact on Hitler when he was controlling the German government later on in life.

After World War I had ended, Hitler being disillusioned with the poor aspects of social life attempted to remain in the military until all remnants of military had been disbanded. He made more as soldier than he did as a private civilian and saw his life much more comfortably in the military than he did in the boarding houses. Like all good things. The German military and finally disbanded and Hitler found himself on the streets of Munich trying to make a living. The Treaty of Versailles had all but crippled the German economy, and led to a much more extreme circumstance where Germans would actually use Deutsch Marks as means to stay warm rather than currency[12]. Germany did show some resilience to the treaties regulations by defaulting on payments to the

---

[12] Kershaw, Ian. *Hitler*. 2nd ed. Vol. 1. New York: W.W. Norton, 1999.

French and British, however having astronomical economic effects among everyday Germans.

By this time Hitler had gained his political voice, and conducted several speeches along with joining a Nationalist Socialist party[13]. Even though he tried to explain that he was the first member in reality he was not, and merely rose in the party due to his ability to have a powerful speech. By this time in Germany, German politics had adopted several parties that fought for control of German government. Social Democrats, religious groups, communist groups, and nationalist groups comprise of the several parties to gain global currency within German. Hitler's uncanny knack and ability to motivate and inspire allowed him to ultimately gain leadership within his own

---

[13] Shirer, William L. *The Rise and Fall of Adolf Hitler*. New York: Random House, 1961.

Nationalists Socialist's party and soon found himself required to turn rhetoric interaction.

The one thing that haunts Hitler throughout his entire life is turning rhetoric into action[14]. In his younger years, he had issues with education, saying that he was going to school and he really wasn't. His later years had much of the same rhetoric to make him popular but will ultimately be as the minds by the eradication of certain social groups such as the Jews. In this instance merely chanting popular political ideology to gain some sort of notoriety but then requiring acting on what is later known as the Beer Hall putsch.

The putsch, like many others of Hitler's plans, is beautiful in idealism but poorly planned by any stretch of imagination. It was a plan to kidnap the

---

14 Shirer, William L. *The Rise and Fall of Adolf Hitler*. New York: Random House, 1961.

three most influential political figures in order to seize control of government. The downside to the plan was that Hitler over estimated the importance of these three individual thinking that the rest of the government and military would fold and fall in line with the party once the rest the leaders had accepted terms with Hitler.

It was quick to see that once the putsch had begun they were going to unravel quickly. Hitler entered the beer hall with other Nazi supporters and took control of Seisser, which was the head of the state police, Kahr, the head of the Bavarian government, and Lossow, which led the German military in the Bavarian region[15]. Each of these men to the back from the beer hall and came to terms with them by stating that he would need the government

---

15 Shirer, William L. *The Rise and Fall of Adolf Hitler*. New York: Random House, 1961.

but these gentlemen would stay in control of their respective departments. Since the Nazis were heavily armed they all agreed.

However, since the remainder of the government takeover was poorly planned military and police were able to fight off all not to aggression and head toward the beer Hall[16]. Knowing that his attempt to overthrow the government had failed and after his arrest all members of the government denying that they had come to terms at any point with Hitler found all leadership members of the Nazi party in court.

It is interesting to see that many of the members of the Nazi party and later members of the government of Germany did not see that Hitler's gift was merely verbal, and he had no real talent for

---

[16] Shirer, William L. *The Rise and Fall of Adolf Hitler*. New York: Random House, 1961.

organization and planning for follow-through. It's hard to believe that an entire country found itself in such dire straits that they blindly followed a man simply because of his ability to verbalize effectively feelings towards the military, financial, and geopolitical circumstances surrounding the country.

Shortly after the failed attempt of the overthrow of the government, Hitler finds itself in a courtroom. Hitler utilizes the circumstances to express his political views and dissolution of the current political climate and circumstance that many other Germans have found them in. Even if Germans did not agree with his ideas, many of them agreed in how they felt after World War I[17]. For some reason, the judge sentenced Hitler to five years imprisonment even though the charges that he faced for treason and recommended sentence of death. Very few thought he

---

[17] Kershaw, Ian. *Hitler*. 2nd ed. Vol. 1. New York: W.W. Norton, 1999.

would be put to death in certain levels because of popularity that Hitler had, however I think you are still thought Hitler would be punished in such a mild manner and the rest of his leadership of the Nazi party virtually released with no punishment would happen.

I think the book points out a very important idea that if Hitler had been sentenced in a more impartial manner, and even more important seeing his sentence carried out completely. History with told of a different Germany after the Great Depression. The attitude of appeasement of the German government after World War I made it possible for people with radical political views to not only gain notoriety, but also to influence, partake, and manipulate all branches of government. I think that even with his tirades in the courtroom, the sentencing that Hitler received and the manner in which he was treated after the attempted overthrow the government had to have even surprised Hitler. At this point, no one could imagine was to come next with the Nazis meteoric rise into power[18].

The meteoric rise of political power of Adolf Hitler can be attributed to two main factors that affected German society after World War I. The first attribute that caused issues in Germany being the treaty of Versailles, and in the second being the Great Depression that caused the downturn and political instability in Germany. Germany with many separate political parties trying to gain political power inside the country found itself relatively stable in the early 1920s. The reason for this was simply because Germany was able to borrow money from other countries in order to sustain itself. One of Germany's main lenders was United States. In 1929, when the

---

[18] Shirer, William L. *The Rise and Fall of Adolf Hitler*. New York: Random House, 1961.

Great Depression began, United States found itself unable to lend money to many different countries. Germany was one of the United States is Maine borrowers prior to the Great Depression found themselves and repairable situations because of their inability to borrow money and not able to produce enough to pay back war reparations[19].

This led Germany into financial catastrophe, which made the German mark worthless. Families were going hungry for the inability to even purchase simple things such as food. This economic situation would in fact fuel smaller political organizations such as the Nazi party to gain power within the government. Hitler simply did one thing to become the leader, his arrogance and unwillingness to settle for anything other than what he wanted allowed him

---

19 Shirer, William L. *The Rise and Fall of Adolf Hitler*. New York: Random House, 1961.

to gain leadership within the Nazi party, and began to vocalize the hardships of the German people and who to blame in order to gain popularity.

The treaty itself was seen as a slap in the face to the German people. Germany needing to surrender territory and best financial reparations as punishment for World War I[20]. Germany became the scapegoat simply because they were the most influential and wealthiest of the axis powers at the conclusion of the war. No one can suggest that Germany was to blame for World War I even though that is exactly how they were treated upon the conclusion of war. This set a dangerous situation and where the very proud people would be punished on the actions of very few.

Along with the financial circumstances of the world found itself in, it laid the foundation in which the Nazi party and in particular Hitler would be able

---

20 Kershaw, Ian. *Hitler*. 2nd ed. Vol. 1. New York: W.W. Norton, 1999.

to gain vast amount of popularity as the voice of national pride and in particular who to blame. The target of Hitler's dissolution was simple, that he simply blamed Communists ideologues and Jews[21]. Hitler portrays the largest of German enemies to be anyone of Jewish descent or communist affiliations. He furthermore promised to not only recapture territory that were lost in Germany after World War I, but create living space out of Western Russian territories.

When Hitler was released from jail and after writing his first book 'My Struggle', he was told by the German military that the only way he would be able to participate is if he swore not to engage in antigovernment behavior, and solely participate in a legal political framework[22]. Hitler agreed privately

---

21 Shirer, William L. *The Rise and Fall of Adolf Hitler*. New York: Random House, 1961.

22 Shirer, William L. *The Rise and Fall of Adolf Hitler*. New York: Random House, 1961.

that the only way to gain complete control the government was through political means. The use of force alone would not create the nationalistic society that he envisioned.

Hitler then begins his campaigning for Nazi officials to gain seats in the Reichstag. All financial contributions to the Nazi party then utilized solely for political gain of the party. When Hitler began this political journey, the social Democrats were the largest and most influential of all political parties inside Germany. Between the various branches of the Nazi party to include the SA, and SS just to name a few[23] . Hitler was able to increase the Nazi party to gain the majority in the Reichstag. The Nazi political machine it with the vast advances in campaigning, such as Hitler traveling by aircraft to do speeches in multiple towns

[23] Kershaw, Ian. *Hitler*. 2nd ed. Vol. 1. New York: W.W. Norton, 1999.

in much shorter time than this competition, found itself in a plateau.

On three separate occasions Hitler himself was invited to participate inside the government but refused to do so because his unwillingness to compromise with Social Democrats. Hitler felt that any positions underneath any other leader of the different political party or even his own would undermine the political advances in his party was able to accomplish into the early 1930s. It was important for Hitler to hold out since his party had been able to capture the majority of the seats in the Reichstag for more influential position.

The SA was still under the notion that Germany would be one through some great victory not just through political pandering. Hitler seized the opportunity of this fringe section of the Nazi party in order to gain trust with the German central government led by Hindenburg[24]. This political peculation paid off because many in the only government but in society saw Hitler as a man who even though had very strong political ideology was a man who is willing to compromise and listen to the rule of law. This cannot be further from the truth, since the tactics that Hitler imposes never suggested that he listened to any authority other than his own ideology.

By 1933 Hitler had risen to the level of Chancellor underneath Hindenburg. He utilized this new position in order to promote and manipulate members of the Nazi party into all aspects of German society to include but not limited to education, military, and religion. Hindenburg himself was merely a leader by title, due to his old age and falling ill. Soon

---

24 Shirer, William L. *The Rise and Fall of Adolf Hitler.* New York: Random House, 1961.

after Hitler's entrance into the central government, Hindenburg dies leaving the charismatic leader of the Nazi party in complete control of Germany[25]. All levels of government leading up to the implementation of Hitler into the central government of Germany was simply due to the fact that Hitler never settled for anything during his time as a political campaigner and requiring all political opponents to conform to him rather than the other way around.

By this time the Nazi party that controlled more than 200 seats in the Reichstag, and control of the executive through Hitler, and membership well into the millions[26]. Hitler's political machine found itself in the middle of a perfect storm of holding out in order to gain as much political capital to influence all aspects of German culture and the ideology of German

25 Shirer, William L. *The Rise and Fall of Adolf Hitler*. New York: Random House, 1961.

26 Kershaw, Ian. *Hitler*. 2nd ed. Vol. 1. New York: W.W. Norton, 1999.

superiority over all other social groups or nationalities. On many instances Hitler promised not to be interested in starting wars but rather assisting in the unemployment of German people, providing defense contracts and construction to what he referred to as building for German defense. Even though many around him and other world leaders saw the military buildup of Germany as too much of a provocative gesture to ignore were not able to influence others to enforce the treaty of Versailles. Germany found itself and in particularly the Nazi regime, with no one to stand against them having free reign of not only their own country but occupying territories and even the invading neighbors justifying it as merely collecting territories belonging to Germany. The rest the world did nothing as Germany took over vast areas of land in Czechoslovakia and eastern France[27].

It was not until September 1, 1939, when Germany invaded Poland that the Allies finally had enough and declared war on Nazi Germany[28].

References:

Kershaw, Ian. *Hitler*. 2nd ed. Vol. 1. New York: W.W. Norton, 1999.

Rhodes, Richard. *Masters of Death: The SS-Einsatzgruppen and the Invention of the Holocaust*. New York: A.A. Knopf, 2002.

Jetzinger, Franz. *Hitler's Youth*. London: Hutchinson, 1958.

Shirer, William L. *The Rise and Fall of Adolf Hitler*. New York: Random House, 1961.

27 Shirer, William L. *The Rise and Fall of Adolf Hitler*. New York: Random House, 1961.

28 Kershaw, Ian. *Hitler*. 2nd ed. Vol. 1. New York: W.W. Norton, 1999.

www.ingramcontent.com/pod-product-compliance
Ingram Content Group UK Ltd.
Pitfield, Milton Keynes, MK11 3LW, UK
UKHW041900190726
13854UKWH00003B/1004

Speak!
Poems by Dogs

Editor, Lisa Kay Adam

Edinburg, Texas.
ISBN 978-1-105-52535-3

Dedicated to the companion animals of the lower Rio Grande Valley.

The editor will donate proceeds from the sale of this edition to the RGV Low Cost Spay / Neuter Clinic of McAllen, Texas.

Felix

Chasing my tail
Chasing the ball
Chasing my tail
Chasing my tail
Chasing my tail
Chasing the ball
Chasing my tail

Help me I can't stop
Chasing my tail

Gimpy

Nights I wake up aching,
I ask myself over and over,
was it worth it? Was it
really so important?
It seemed so at the time.
Those speeding metal giants
seemed irresistible. They smelled

like something fetid,
something burning.
I couldn't wait
to catch one. I thought
I could sharpen my teeth
on the grindstone
of their spinning wheels.

It wasn't worth it but
what did I know? Every day
every day, same yard,
same food thrown in a pan,
same man walking past
with a pat on the head.

Only the metal animals
seemed alive.

Boss-Hogg

Sofa, chair leg, corner, table.
Sofa, chair leg, corner, table.
Bedspread, curtain, doorway.

That's my beat, yeah,
That's mine, but HE,
he's trying to mess
with what's mine,
sprays some violet-puke
on my scent,
pours out some language
that would make
a lesser dog's fur curl.

I say, "F__ you, too, dude."
You said you wanted
another guy around the house.
Well,
Here
I
AM!

Trixie

I love you?

I love you!

I love you I love you I love
you I love you I love you I
love you I love you I love you
I love you I LOVE YOU I LOVE
YOU I LOVE YOU.

I love you.

I love you?

Female #28

Poo poo poo
I lick their poo
when they are born
but there is still
poo
everywhere
all the time
I don't know how
many
there have been
babies
I have babies always
there is always poo

Goldie

My owners say: She's good
with kids. I take that to mean
they like my tolerance
for these small crazed animals
that run the house.
What choice do I have?
Just when things calm down--
no more crying, biting, tugging,
and stink that even a dog can't take--
they produce another one.

Now there are four.
I admit, the oldest is starting
to become a good dog, of sorts.
We take long walks together.
We sit together on the grass
and lean against each other.
He has a good smell, lately.
I guess we can grow old
together.

Sharp-Dressed Man

Who the hell cares what my name is?
They only care about my looks.
Little sweaters, hoodies,
leather vests, bandanas,
bow ties, hats
that smash my ears.
Itchy, irritating, irksome,
ignominious.
It's true I'm small and shiver-y,
but leave me some dignity.

A little metal cage,
a little leather cage slung on a shoulder:
they take me out and pass me around
as if I had no legs, as if I couldn't
outrun any god-damn Great Dane
given a really good head start.

Well, I don't know their names, either.
There was one with long dark hair
who I thought might be The One,
but she two-timed me
with some trashy mop
of a dog, and then passed
me to a blonde,
who gave me to this new one.
She still stuffs me into sweaters
like a sausage, makes my
joints hurt. Doesn't she know

I'm an old man now?

Bitsy

I was the one who never got a teat,
the little dwindling velvet bag of bones.
At first, I was glad when the pushy fat ones
were taken, plucked from the side
of our mother.
More for me.
But then even the ones
who let me cuddle
disappeared.

It was only me and mom
running around the cage.

They should see me now,
sitting with my plump belly
on my own plump
velvet pillow.

Dog

It is exactly twenty-two paces to the
It is exactly twenty-two paces to the
It is exactly twenty-two paces to the
There is that black cat I am going to
There is that black cat I am going to
It is exactly twenty-two paces to the
Here comes the mailman I am going
It is exactly twenty-two paces to the
IT IS EXACTLY TWENTY-TWO PACES
My chain tastes like metallic bones
of dead cats I want to kill mailmen
It is exactly twenty-two paces to the
end some day I will eat every chain.

Fargo / Sebastian

I know I have it good. She feeds me.
She lets me sit beside her and watch
tv. But every day, the same window,
the same birds, the same walk
around the block. Once I had

a different life, different name, and different humans,
a pair that had no home except a home
that moved, and they took me with them.
I rode with them in the broad nose
behind the glass, my feet seemed to eat
the miles without ever touching ground.

We went different places, sometimes stayed
a day, a week, a month.
When they let me out, the smells
were glorious and exotic
and feral: strange fruit,
strange forests, strange animals.
The lure of the smells

was my downfall. I followed one too long,
too deep into the trail, and then
and then and then where was I?
There was a road, and a woman
who picked me up
but put me in the back seat.

It was my fault. I shouldn't
have given her my sad dog look.
I should have kept searching.
But I thought she would take me
back to my pair. I thought
all humans knew each other.

Mendigo

I'm not, strictly, a junkyard dog.
No one keeps me here, but I like
the mice that hide between
the grocery baskets and the tires.

I like the taqueria down the street,
where the people throw me scraps
and call me Mendigo, beggar,
which isn't, strictly, true.
I don't beg, I wait.

It's a good life. I like
the cool grass in the ditch
during summers. I like
the taste of roasting meat
at the backyard barbecues
that I'm not, exactly, invited to.

But, it's lonesome. There used to be
three of us, a pack, but one collided
with a car (I still veer around the spot)
and one ate a rat that made him sick.
I don't like to remember that.

But it's a good life. I roam,
I wait, I watch. I think
people could give me something
besides scraps and bones,
but what that would be,
exactly,
I don't know.

Nessa

Woo baby, take me
to the park, 'cuz
I am fine.
I got my pink bow,
I got my pink nails,
I got my pink collar,
I got my poodle cut.
I am hot to trot,
I'm bitchin'
Pick me up
and
love on me.

Bad Boy Bennie

That's just my AKC name.
I'm really milquetoast.
I like my Milk Bones,
I like my plaid blankie,
I like my belly rubbed.
I could have been named
something like,
Happy Hanover
or Sappy Stu,
but who wants
a stud named Stu?
Even in the dog world,
the nice guy never
gets the girl.

Lady

I know I'm not faithful
the way a good dog should be.
This house has everything:
a big porch with a barrel of food
that hardly ever runs out,
a big bowl of water that hardly
ever runs low, a box of sheets
and blankets that I dig in
to my heart's content, and a ball
that I nose around on the porch
until it falls off and I go get it.

This house has everything,
but I'm unfaithful. I'm unfaithful!
Surely they know! Don't they see
the big gap underneath the fence,
the big hollow that I've wallowed out
from slithering under, day after day
that I'm unfaithful? Why don't they
do something to stop me? Oh!
Do something to stop me!

The other house has nothing.
Nothing! It's got no porch,
no box, no barrel, no bowl.
Just a hard bench by the door.
All it's got is this girl.
And if I sit long enough on the bench,
this girl, this girl...scratches me,
oh, oh, oh...behind the ear.

Oh! I'm unfaithful! Why
don't they do something
to stop me?

Mignon

This is my world:
cool, cool, cool, warm, hot,
cool, HOT, hot, hot, cool....
I don't know how else to explain it.
It's what I've learned the year I've been here.
Certain places are just fine, she's cool,
I'm cool. Other places,
I'm in hot water. All day long

I navigate from space to space.
Watch out, Mignon, I tell myself,
play it straight and narrow, but of course,
I'm always learning new places where I'm
not supposed to be. I caught it hard

at the kitchen trash and the bathroom mat,
and the thought of her big luscious bed
with the delicious pillows still leaves me
feeling scorched. But I'm cool

with my metal crate, the blue blanket
on the chair, the food bowls on the floor,
and the last fourteen feet of yard, but only
past the yellow flowers. There, it's not

cool or hot, but everything mixed together
in a good jumble of cool grass, warm breeze,
hot sun. I roll, I stretch, I sniff, and I run
around and around and around, but only
past the yellow flowers.

Chulo

She calls me Handsome, and she talks to me
all day long. It's Chulo this and Chulo that,
and sometimes we play a game where
the more she says my name,
the more I lick her--hands and feet,
and if I'm quick, cheeks, chin, and nose.
The opposite of hungry isn't full; it's this
turning-inside-out feeling I have then. It's strange

how it started with a crust of bread,
and a few stale tortillas smeared with beans
left in a shiny pan that scared me,
but I ate them when she turned her back.

Then she started staying to watch me eat.
That scared me. It reminded me of what
a beggar I really was. But I was hungry,
and she seemed old and slow.
The more I ate, the more she fed me.

One day

she held out a chicken bone.

I came close and took one end.
She didn't let go--tug, tug, tug--
and then she turned loose with a stream
of words so fluttery and soft it reminded me
of the birds I used to watch in the junkyard tree.
It was Chulo this and Chulo that,
but I didn't know, then,
that she meant me.

Sister

If he's not hanging on my ears,
he's chewing on my tail,
eating my food, stealing my toys.

Every dogs needs a playmate,
she said. Now where would she get
such a cockamamie idea?
Did I give her any indication
that I was less than one-hundred-percent
for-sure dee-lighted
at being her Number One
and Only
Dog?

Now I don't even have the dignity
of my name. It used to be
Delilah. Now it's Sister, as in
Sister, be good to little brother,
and Sister, you can share that toy.

Better that then when she calls me
Little Mama, as if I would ever give birth
to this squirming monster she brought home.
He's only any good when he's asleep.

67.2012

I wish I could remember
more. I wish I could remember
where I started, but the howling
confuses me.
I remember people driving
away and roads and roads
and roads. I remember
people's white teeth
flashing at me, people's hands
extended, gesturing, throwing
things at me. I remember
the taste of cardboard boxes
soaked with grease. I remember cold.
I remember the wire noose,
another road, a cage,
and now this howling
from the dogs
coming and going,
coming and going
around me, each
in its own cage of noise.
Where are they going?
Where am I going?

I never thought I would want, so much,
to be back on the roads
that go on and on
endlessly.

Cletus

Speak! Speak! they kept saying.
For a long time, I didn't understand.
Their other commands had made more sense--
    Sit, Come, Down, Stay.
But Speak? They never told me
what they wanted me to say or why.

Okay, I finally realized a full-throated reply
was all it took to make them laugh and smile.
But they wouldn't like it if they really knew
what I was howling:
Foooooooools! Fooooooools!
Lovable fools.

Bud

We met beneath the bridge.
I saw the light and came close.
He called me over, and cut me loose
from the rope that I'd been dragging.
Since then I've never left him

and I never will, even though
I hate this life we lead.
The bridge and the abandoned buildings
where we stay aren't so bad;
at least they seem safe.

But the long days scare me and wear me out,
the walking and walking, and worse,
the busy corners where I sit while
he weaves between the cars with
his sign and can. The smell of cars

never leaves us. It's in our nose,
our mouths, our guts.
But I haven't gone hungry once
while I've been with him, even when
I've heard his stomach growl.

I would say I'm a burden,
but I help keep him warm,
and I wake him up from the dreams
that make him flinch and kick.
I lick his face, he throws a heavy arm
around me, and we go back to sleep.

I'll never leave him.

Sponger

Something went haywire with my human
about a year ago. Now he jumps around;
he flings his arms and legs to music;
he drags me on long fast walks;
he keeps offering me odd food,
like tiny carrots, hmph.
What happened to the French fries
          we used to share?

His fat warm lap had been
my favorite place to nap.
Now he's scrawny and I'm reduced
to sleeping on the sofa.

Foxer

Rubber bones take like shit.
No, that's wrong. Shit tastes good.
Rubber bones are only
for those idiot pups who chew up
shoes and books and pencils.

I am not one of those.

My humans wish to think otherwise.
They offer these rubber bones,
and tennis balls, and some limp
fuzzy bag they call Mousy,
which I occasionally give
an obligatory shake.
But I know the difference,
and they know I know the difference,
and they hate it.

They hate it when I linger too late
outside at night. They know
I am listening, smelling, probing,

waiting...
for the delectable moment
when I can sink teeth through
fur and flesh and little bones like straw,

waiting...
for the exquisite squeal that snaps
my jaws shut like a steel trap.

Then let them yell at me all they want,
let them say that's nasty and I'm bad.
Eh...they don't offend me.
They don't deter me.

I know what I am.

Ranger

This man and I have always been together.
What a match we were, large and swift and strong.
We were like two trees that held up the sky.
In the morning, when we got up,
he from his bed, me from mine,
we made the sun rise. We made the day
pass beneath our feet, walking, working in the pasture.
And when we tired out, the night would come for us.
We carried the world lightly.

But now the world is getting heavier and heavier.
I see it shrinking him and bending him low
over the wooden stick he uses now to walk.
And I feel it, too, a heavy weight that bears
down on my back legs and makes them ache.

What will happen when one of us
            can no longer walk?
How will the other hold up our world?

If the world won't let up, then
let the world crush us together.
We once were trees.
We can also be stones.

Ladybug

It all happened so fast.
The girl followed me to the house
and rang the bell. They all stood outside
and talked and looked at me. I was sure
they were saying I was unfaithful.
But the next thing I know,
I've got this leash on, and off we go
down the road, the girl and me.
I looked back once, wondering,
why didn't they do something to stop me?
But they'd gone inside the house.

The girl still had the scratch.
Oh, the scratch! Behind my ear,
beneath my chin, and that spot on my belly
that makes my back leg kick.

And, it turns out that, all along,
the girl had a ball.
and a bowl of water,
and a bowl of food,
and a bed big enough
for both of us. Who knew

you could have it all?

Gracie

Most days my human seems so large.
He gives everything, good or bad:
praise and petting, punishment (sometimes),
food and water. Everything
seems warm when he's present.
A cool shadow falls everywhere
when he's gone. The rest of the world
seems small around his margins.

But some days we go to that place by a lake,
and I realize that he and I are both small pups
beside the hugeness of the sky and fields,
the far-awayness of the trees and sun,
and the good taste and smell of everything.

On those days, I don't know which is better:
the bounding away from him to chase a bird,
with the wind licking my face as I run so fast,
or the leaping return, when he grows
from a dot on the edge of the world
to a man holding his arms wide for me.
I like to zip past his fingertips, skid,
and then turn back with a bound
that tumbles us both. Then it's my turn
to lick and yelp in joy.

I try to fill the sky with my happy barking,
try to touch everything I can with my paws
and taste everything I can with my tongue.
My human smiles and looks at me
in a way that says he knows,
says he's glad to step aside awhile
to show me this bigness,
this wonderfulness, this good world.

(My dog's poem)

(My dog's poem)

(My dog's poem)

www.ingramcontent.com/pod-product-compliance
Ingram Content Group UK Ltd.
Pitfield, Milton Keynes, MK11 3LW, UK
UKHW041900190726
13854UKWH00003B/1005

9 781105 525353